CW00402809

Memories of CONSETT

COUNTY DURHAM BOOKS

The compilers of this book have endeavoured to contact and seek permission from the copyright holders of all the photographs used herein. If we have inadvertently used a picture without permission we would be grateful if the copyright holder would contact us so that we can make the proper acknowledgement in any future editions.

Front cover: Consett Front Street looking towards the Steel Works.

© County Durham Books, 2005

All rights reserved. No part of this publication may be reproduced, stored in a retrieval system, or transmitted in any form or by any means, electronic, mechanical, photocopying or otherwise, without the prior permission of the publisher.

Published by County Durham Books, 2005

County Durham Books is the imprint of Durham County Council

ISBN 1897585837

Memories of **CONSETT**

Memories are very precious.

Often they are related to an area - for example, where we live, where we went to school, where we fell in love - but whether you are new to Consett or your family have lived here for generations, we are sure you'll be fascinated by the 'memories' contained in this book.

As you are taken on a nostalgic walk around Consett and the surrounding areas you'll notice the dramatic changes to the old buildings and physical layout of our area. The demise of the steel and coal industries and the subsequent financial investment into the region has resulted in a vast difference to working and living conditions, in particular, a cleaner and healthier environment.

Consett Library has played a crucial social and community role in the town. From the early days of lending enjoyable reading books and educational support (in hushed surroundings) to our modern-day services offering everything from DVDs to free computer and internet access - as well as reading books and educational support - we have been a means of bringing the community together in events and activities and supporting and maintaining memories of our local historic heritage.

This book has drawn on our library archive material but could not have been produced without the wholehearted support of 'Consett people'.

The staff at Consett library would like to thank everyone who has assisted in collecting our memories together. A special 'Thank you' to all who donated their photographs and offered their time and help.

The original Consett war memorial situated along Aynsley Terrace is where we begin our memory walk into the town centre.

Early view of Victoria Road. No library in the distance, just rows of houses.

Next is a view looking up John Street onto Medomsley Road. On the right is the old telephone exchange which is now the County Court. Can you remember the buses being parked down John Street?

View of terraced houses where the bus station is now situated. The people on the seat are sitting where Consett Library is presently sited.

View of old Consett bus station showing the rows of terraced houses which are now demolished.

View of a deserted Consett bus station. Burrells was a popular dropping-off point to get your sweets before going on a long bus journey or to the 'pictures'.

The Clock at the bottom of the bus station was a regular meeting point. Note the Plaza cinema in the background.

Lower market square, Victoria Road with Lloyds Bank and Front Street in background. Donaghy's fruit and vegetable shop on the corner as it still is today.

How could we forget the famous red dust of Consett drifting over the town centre?

We've reached Front Street, which is still recognisable today, although sadly Pattinsons is no longer there. On the opposite corner above Woolworths is the Freemasons pub and then the Ballroom. On the following page is a very early view of the Freemasons Arms, Consett.

Freemasons Arms public house on Front Street.

View of Front Street, showing Doggarts, which was a well-known department store in Consett for many years. On the next page is a more recent view of Front Street.

Front Street, looking towards the steel works. You can see where Doggarts used to be on the right of this picture and the more recent up-dated Doggarts on the left. Consett Iron Company, later the British Steel Corporation, can be clearly seen in the background.

Very old view of Consett Town Hall on Front Street. Can you see the terraced houses known as Company Rows where Wetherspoons now stands.

The old Consett Town Hall burnt down on 4th May 1906. The police sergeant in the photograph was Mr. Carruthers.

After World War 2, many new houses were built in Consett and the surrounding area. This is Stanley Gardens in Consett before additional housing was built.

Travelling towards Leadgate from Front Street we come to Sherburn Terrace. We believe this is a photograph of General Booth visiting Consett Salvation Army Citadel. Can you spot how many different modes of transport are in this picture?

Hat and Feather public house, still going strong today.

Early view of St. Ives Road, Leadgate, near Consett.

Can you remember the Primitive Methodist Church at the bottom of Park Road, Consett?

Early view of Durham Road, Blackhill. The Methodist Church is on the right hand side.

Soldiers on horseback with a heavy loaded cart parading down Blackhill bank.

Early view of Benfieldside Road, before extensive house building.

Staff proudly pose for a photograph outside Consett Co-operative store at Shotley Bridge.

Very early view of the Chelmsford Hotel, Ebchester.

Before automobiles, the Venture stage coach was a very exclusive mode of transport. The view over the countryside must have been wonderful!

This is a view of the Stanefordham, now known as the Castleside Inn. Apart from the steamroller, horse and cart was the regular form of transport.

Picture of the original bandstand in Blackhill park. The new bandstand in the park today is still a cultural meeting point for many forms of entertainment and celebration for everyone in Consett.

'Fame at last!' It was great to have your photograph in the 'Consett Guardian'. For many years the Consett Guardian Chronicle office was the place to go and look at, or buy, photographs of local events and celebrations.

This is a photograph of a First Communion at St. Patrick's Church, Consett. Do you recognise anyone?

Over the years there have been many churches in Consett, and those that are still there today are great meeting points for the community. This is an interesting sketch of the proposed Consett Primitive Methodist Church which was built along Middle Street where Inshops now stands.

This is an early view of Christ Church, Consett. A lot of the original decoration is no longer visible.

Consett Church of England School's 'Good attendance' presentation on 22nd October, 1923. Front row on the left is Robbie Blemings, who worked in Doggarts for many years and was well-known in Consett.

Catholic Travel Association trip to Lourdes in 1972.

This is a photograph of Consett citizens choir with their conductor Mr. William Westgarth. The choir is still going today and is well loved in Consett for their concerts and Christmas pantomimes.

Victory Street tea party - Buddle Street, Gill Street and Forster Street, Consett.

Chapel Christening Day at Leadgate 1928. Some of the babies pictured are Margaret and Olive Proctor, John Day, Bob Craig, Lorna McKinnell and Ernest Jeffrey.

The Rex cinema was a popular place of entertainment. It was one of three cinemas in Consett. Sadly it was burnt down and the site is now occupied by the current Job Centre.

Styles may have changed but dancing was, and still is, a much loved pastime. This is a photograph of a barn dance at Castleside in the 1950s.

The staff of Collinsons were well-known for their fashion shows.

Derwent Valley morris men, 1958.

Stella Hayley, 'Miss Highgate 1954', with other competitors at the Highgate Show, Bridgehill.

Evening presentation by Mr. William Westgarth, Mr. Dougie Wray, Miss Gladys Maddison and Councillor Mrs. Mahon to Stella Haley (Miss Highgate 1954) at Consett Dance Hall, Middle Street. ('The Pally')

School kitchen staff, Sherburn Terrace, Consett. Approximately 1947.

1950 Benfieldside senior school sports day. Do you recognise yourself?

Benfieldside senior school folk dance group, August 1972.

Mother and baby group, Christ Church, Consett pictured Christmas 1968.

Benfieldside seniors football club 1952.

Benfieldside netball team 1972/1973.

A class from Leadgate Junior School 1965

Wonderful view of the Gill Bridge. The railways were not only a vital passenger service but also supported the local steel and coal industries in the area.

Mineworkers from the Victory Pit, Delves Lane.

Templetown coke and bi-product plant.

Local steelmen having a well earned break at Consett Iron Company. Do you recognise anyone?

The last Steel Works apprentices at Consett to gain their indentures before the Steel Works closed.

Management staff at Consett Steel Works.

Consett Iron Company - Works Electric (Armature winding section) 1958.